CULTURE IN ACTION

Photography

Liz Miles

Chicago, Illinois

www.heinemannraintree.com
Visit our website to find out
more information about
Heinemann-Raintree books.

To order:

☎ Phone 888-454-2279

💻 Visit www.heinemannraintree.com
to browse our catalog and order online.

Edited by Louise Galpine and Rachel Howells
Designed by Kimberly Miracle and Betsy Wernert
Original illustrations © Capstone Global Library Ltd.
Illustrated by kja-artists.com and Medi-mation (p. 16)
Picture research by Hannah Taylor and Kay Altwegg
Originated by Dot Gradations Ltd.
Printed and Bound in the United States
by Corporate Graphics

13 12 11 10 09
10 9 8 7 6 5 4 3 2 1

Library of Congress Cataloging-in-Publication Data
Miles, Liz.
  Photography / Liz Miles.
    p. cm. -- (Culture in action)
  Includes bibliographical references and index.
  ISBN 978-1-4109-3400-0 (hc) -- ISBN 978-1-4109-3417-8
(pb) 1. Cameras--Juvenile literature. 2. Photography--
Technique--Juvenile literature. I. Title.
  TR250.M55 2008
  771.3--dc22
                            2008054322

Acknowledgments

The author and publishers are grateful to the following for
permission to reproduce copyright material: Alamy pp. **16** top
(© vanneilbob), **18** (© I. Glory), **20** (© vario images GmbH &
Co.KG); ©Andy Goldsworthy p. **5**; ©Capstone Publishers
pp. **17**, L-R, **22**, and **23, top to bottom** (Karon Dubke); Corbis
pp. **24** (Frans Lanting), **28** (Leo Mason); Getty Images pp. **19**
(Time Life Pictures/ National Archives/ Ansel Adams), **25**
(Hulton Archive/ Ernst Haas), **26** (David McNew), **29** (Time
Life Pictures/ Jeffrey L. Rotman); PA Photos pp. **4** (DPA), **12**
(Gareth Copley), **21** (AP Photo/Nick Ut); Science & Society
Picture Library pp. **6** (Science Museum), **7**, **8**, **9**, and **10**
(National Media Museum).

Icon and banner images supplied by Shutterstock: © Alexander
Lukin, © ornitopter, © Colorlife, and © David S. Rose.

Cover photograph of sneaky photographer getting his shot,
reproduced with permission of istockphoto (@ PeskyMonkey).

We would like to thank Brian Payne, Jackie Murphy, and
Nancy Harris for their invaluable help in the preparation of
this book.

Every effort has been made to contact copyright holders
of any material reproduced in this book. Any omissions
will be rectified in subsequent printings if notice is given to
the publisher.

Contents

Some words are printed in bold, **like this**. You can find out what they mean by looking in the glossary on page 30.

Photographs Around Us

Photographs are everywhere—newspapers, magazines, books, postcards, and **galleries**. A photographer takes the photographs you see by looking through a camera, and pressing a button.

What's in a photograph?

Anything can be in a photograph. Newspaper photographs range from shots of sporting events to horrific pictures of war scenes. Magazines might show smiling celebrities or a faraway place. Books show all kinds of photographs, too.

Being famous means that you often have to face photographers who want to take your picture.

Medical workers take a different kind of photograph. They take x-rays that photograph **organs** and bones in the body. Astronomers use telescopes to photograph the stars. Artists take photographs of their art, such as sculptures. Like paintings, artistic photographs are often displayed in **galleries**.

The artist Andy Goldsworthy took this photograph of his outdoor sculpture *Rowan Leaves and Hole*. The sculpture of leaves will not last long, but the photograph will.

An exciting life

Professional photographers have to take good photographs every day to earn a living. **Amateur** photographers can have fun taking **snapshots** of their family and friends. Others take their hobby more seriously. They practice hard and take part in competitions.

Multiskilled

Photographers need many skills. They need to have an artistic eye. This means they have to be able to see what makes an attractive photograph or a good **composition**. They also need to know how to use a camera. There are other important tools, too, such as **lenses**, lighting equipment, and computers. A lens sharpens an image.

Greek origins

The word "photography" comes from the Greek words *photos*, meaning "light," and *graphos*, which means "writing."

Camera Beginnings

A picture is a lasting reminder of an event or person. For thousands of years, the only pictures people had were drawings, paintings, **prints** (paper images), and carvings. In 1824 this changed when the world's first photograph was taken.

Camera obscura

In the fourth and fifth centuries, people started to find out how to create photographs. They noticed that if light passed through a pinhole into a darkened room, it made an upside-down image on the opposite wall. By the 1500s, **portable**, box-shaped versions of these rooms were made. They were called camera obscuras. They were portable and had a pinhole on one side.

During the 1500s, a **lens** and mirror were put in camera obscuras. The lens made the image clearer. The mirror reflected the image in the box onto the top. This made it easier to see. People could also now trace the image to make a drawing.

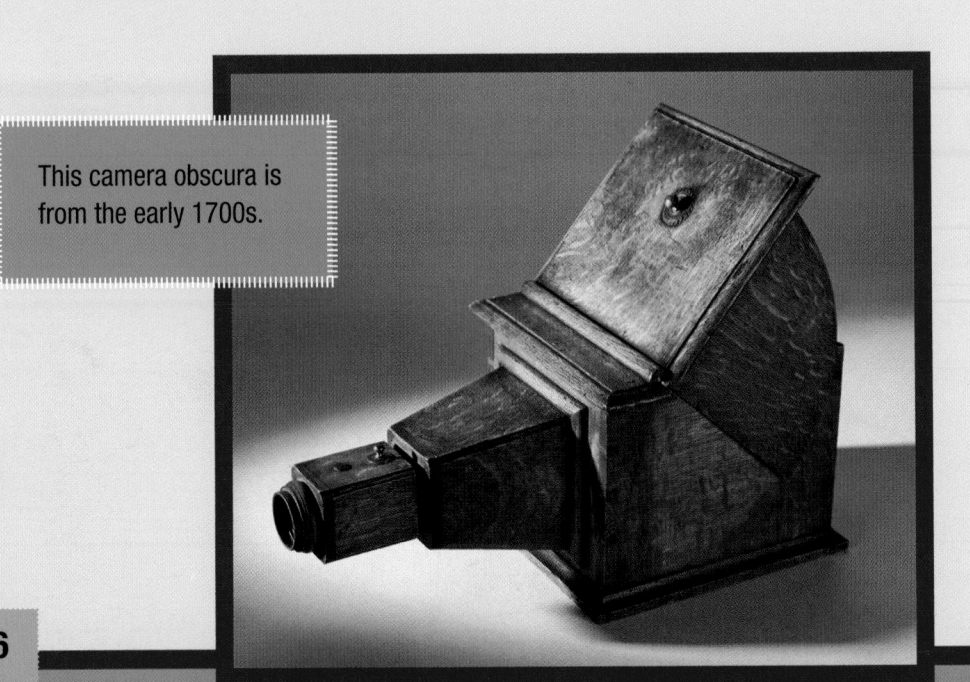

This camera obscura is from the early 1700s.

6

The first photograph

In 1826 French inventor Joseph Niépce came up with a new idea. He covered a piece of coated metal plate with soft tar and put it in the back of a camera obscura. He used the lens to shine an image onto it. The tar hardened into the image. It was the first real photograph. The fuzzy photograph showed a pigeon house and a barn.

Daguerreotype

Another French inventor named Louis Daguerre improved Niépce's method. Daguerre's photographs were more detailed. They usually showed portraits of people. These photographs were called daguerreotypes. But there was still only one copy of each image.

This is the oldest surviving daguerreotype photograph, made in 1837.

From positive to negative

In the 1830s, English inventor William Henry Fox Talbot was the first person to take **negative** images. These are pictures that have the light and dark tones reversed. The negatives were useful. Each negative could be made into more than one **positive print** of each image. This meant that the light and dark tones were not reversed. A lot of copies (prints) of one photograph could now be made. Photographs could now appear in newspapers, books, and magazines for the first time!

The term

Astronomer Sir John Herschel called Talbot's invention of printing positive images from a negative "photography." It was a term that stuck!

In the 1800s, you had to sit still for 30 seconds or more to have a photograph taken.

Wet and dry plates

Until the 1870s, photographic **plates** were "wet." They were sticky and coated in **chemicals**. Photographers had to carry around the plates and chemicals, plus their big cameras. The plates had to be **developed** (made into photographs) within 10 minutes of an image being taken. So photographers had to travel around with their own **darkroom**. This was a place where a photograph could be developed. In 1871 "dry plates" were made. These were less messy, easier to use, and did not have to be developed right away.

The first color photograph ever taken was of a plaid ribbon.

Color

For many years people tried but failed to take color photographs. So black-and-white photographs were often touched up or painted with watercolors or inks. The first plates that took color photographs were made in 1907. Modern color film was first sold in 1935. It was known as Kodachrome.

Anyone could take a **snapshot** with a Kodak Brownie.

Photographic film

In 1884 **photographic film** was invented. It is a **light-sensitive** paper that records images. It replaced heavy plates and could be rolled up to fit into smaller cameras.

In 1888 the first camera with rolled film went on sale. The buyers were told, "You press the button, we do the rest." The buyer could take their photographs, then send the film to be developed. Taking photographs was easier, and people did not have to sit still for a long time to have their photograph taken.

At first, these cameras were too expensive for most people to buy. Then, in 1900, the first affordable camera went on sale—the Kodak Brownie. It was an instant success.

Over time, camera technology improved. For example, an electronic **flash** was introduced in 1931 to make photographs brighter. **Digital cameras** went on sale in 1990. Within 14 years, digital cameras were more popular than film cameras.

Match the mood

What's in a photograph? Of course, there is the **subject** (such as a person or a view), but there will also be a mood. The aim of this activity is to find music to match the mood of photographs.

You will need:

- a selection of old photographs (black and white if possible)
- a newspaper and scissors
- various CDs of different types of music (classical and pop, if possible).

Steps to follow:

1. Choose a photograph from your selection, or cut out a photograph from a newspaper.

2. Play two or three different pieces of music as you look at the photograph. Does the different music make you see certain details in the photograph? Does quiet music make you notice that a person is looking away? Does loud music make you notice a dark cloud looming in the sky?

3. Decide on the main mood of the photograph. Match a piece of music to it.

4. Write a title for the photograph to fit its mood.

5. Show your photograph to a friend. Play the music you chose. Can your friend think of any other music that could go with your photograph?

How Do Cameras Work?

The body of a film camera is a lightproof box—a sealed box that light cannot get into. When the button is pressed to take a picture, the shutter (a kind of door) opens for less than a second. This lets light from the **subject** pass through a hole (the **aperture**) into the camera. A **lens** focuses the image onto **light-sensitive** film in the back of the camera.

Some useful definitions

Depth of field—the area (part) of an image that is in focus

Focus—to make a photograph clear and not fuzzy. Turning the camera lens does this.

Focal length—the distance from the center of a lens to its focal point. This is the point at which the image of a distant object is in focus.

A fast shutter speed on a camera allows a photographer to take a split-second image of a fast-moving person or object.

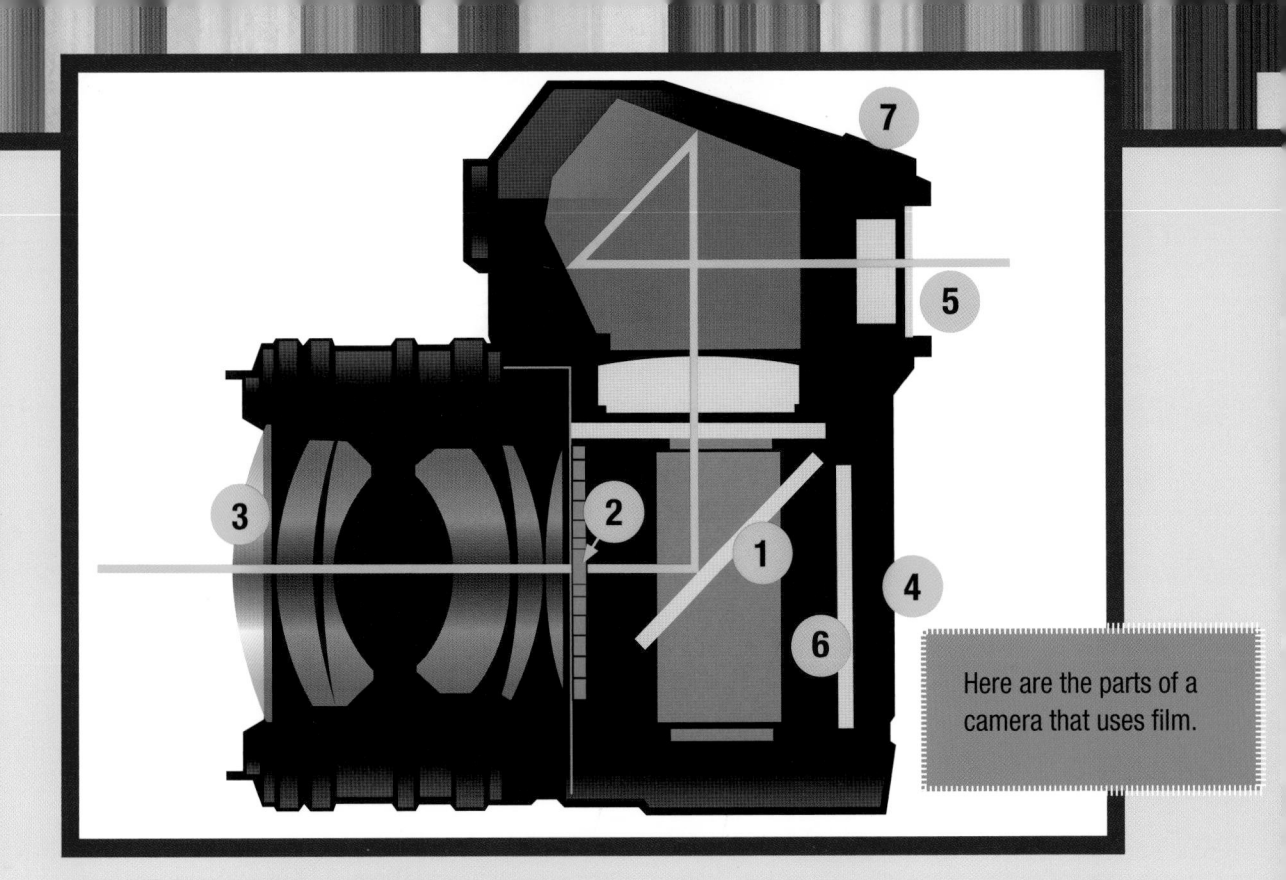

Here are the parts of a camera that uses film.

1. *Mirror:* A piece of glass that reflects light coming through the lens and allows you to see the image through the **viewfinder**.

2. *Aperture:* A ring around the aperture can be widened or narrowed. This controls the **exposure** (how much light gets in).

3. *Lens:* A camera lens is made up of several pieces of glass. Turning the lens can sharpen or blur the image. The lens controls how far you can zoom in or out on the image. Lenses can focus on something close to the camera, or something far away.

4. *Film:* This is what you put in the camera to take a photograph. It usually comes in a roll. After you take a picture you move the film on. This allows you to take another photograph on the same roll.

5. *Viewfinder:* When you look through this small opening, you can see your subject.

6. *Shutter:* This works like a window and only opens when you push the shutter button on your camera. When the shutter opens, this allows the image you see through the viewfinder to be captured on the roll of film.

7. *Shutter button:* When you press the shutter button, it opens and closes the shutter and takes the photograph.

Do you see what the camera sees?

When you look through the **viewfinder** of certain types of cameras, you see exactly the same image that goes through the lens. This image will be on the film and printed photograph. To get a perfect photograph, it is important to see the photograph you are taking. You need to see what the camera sees.

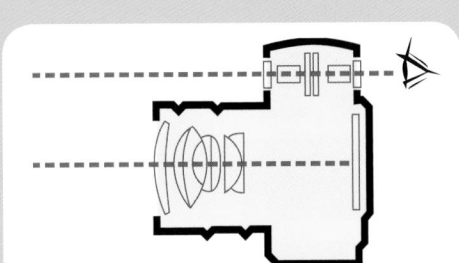

Viewfinder camera

The viewfinder is at the top, so you look through the top of the camera. But the light from the image passes through the lens, which is lower. You do not see what the camera sees.

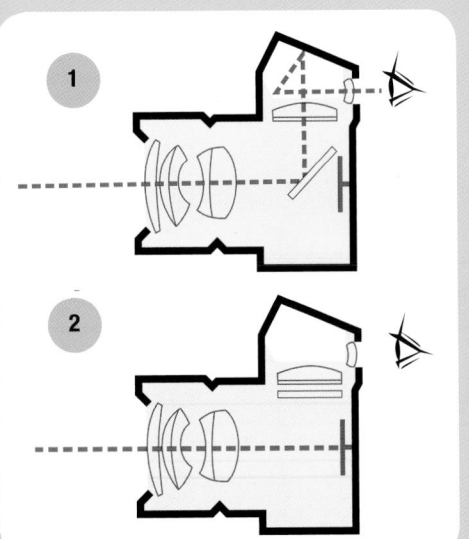

Single-lens reflex camera

Even though the viewfinder is above the lens, you still see the image that is coming through the lens, right up to the second the picture is taken. A mirror reflects the light of the image up to a glass block and into the viewfinder (picture 1). When you press the shutter button to take the picture, the mirror flips up. Light then passes to the film (picture 2).

Digital camera

You see what the camera sees if the digital camera has an **LCD screen**. An LCD screen is a large screen on the back of the camera.

How does a digital camera work?

Like film cameras, **digital cameras** have a body, a shutter, and a lens. But digital cameras do not capture an image on a roll of film.

Digital cameras capture the image on a **light sensor**. The sensor picks up the patterns of light from the image. The patterns of light are changed into **digital signals**. The signals are stored in the camera on a tiny **memory card**.

Pixels

Digital photographs are made up of millions of squares of color (called **pixels**). The more pixels there are, the sharper the picture. Usually 200 pixels per inch is enough for a good **print**.

From camera to printer

Computers and printers can "read" the digital signals on a memory card and turn them into images. How do you get the images from the camera to a computer or printer? To do this the memory card is taken from the camera and plugged into the computer or printer. It is also possible to pass the images down a cable from the camera to a computer.

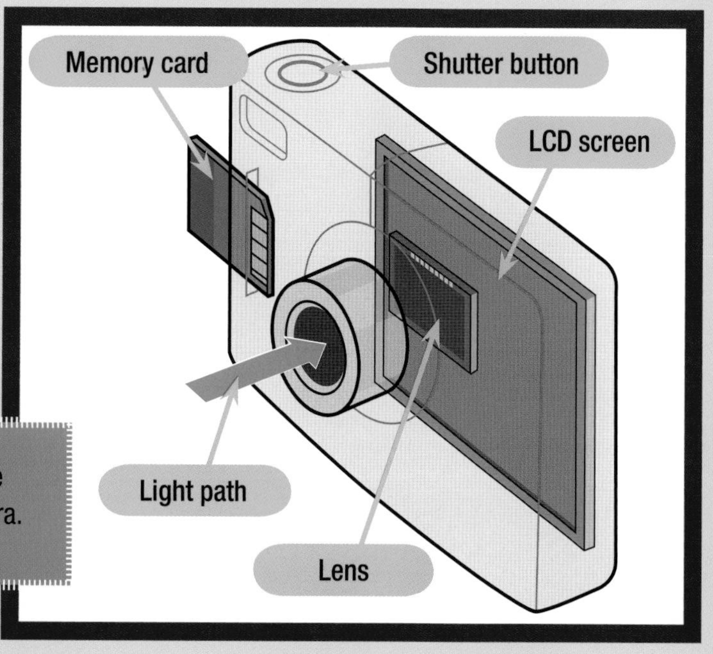

This diagram shows the inside of a digital camera.

Memory card

Shutter button

LCD screen

Light path

Lens

Depth of field

If you take a photograph of a crowded beach, only a part of the scene will look sharp. This area is called the depth of field. To get a bigger depth of field (so that more of the picture is in focus), photographers make the camera's **aperture** smaller. Another way to get a bigger depth of field is to change the lens.

Filter and flash

White light is made up of all the colors in a rainbow. Filters can block out some of the colors to make other colors bolder, such as a very blue sky. A **flash** makes extra light. People often use their camera's flash indoors and at night. However, it can also be useful to lighten shadowy areas in daytime shots.

A camera lens gathers light rays from outside and focuses them into an image on the camera's film or sensor.

Fashion shoots and mug shots

Fashion shoot

Work with a friend on a fashion photo shoot.

You will need:

• some interesting-looking clothes

• a digital camera.

Steps to follow:

1. Find a well-lit room. You may need to use the flash on the camera.

2. The photographer should guide the model on the best poses to show off the clothes.

3. Take photographs from different angles and distances.

4. Print the photographs.

5. Make a page for a fashion magazine. Write captions and an article describing the clothing.

How to take photographs of people:

• Make sure the person is relaxed
• Don't always insist on a smile
• Check the pose—make sure the person's hands are relaxed
• Find a good setting
• Experiment with props (capture the person doing an activity such as painting).

Mug shots

Work with a friend to make a sequence of portraits. The model should show a different emotion for each shot. Can your friends guess the emotion?

A happy face   A confused face   A sad face   A surprised face

In the Darkroom

Some photographers **develop** and print their own photographs. The processes they use are described below. They take place in a **darkroom**, where there is no daylight. It would ruin the **light-sensitive** equipment.

From camera to gallery

1. In complete darkness, the film is taken out of the camera.

2. It is put in a developing tank.

3. **Chemicals** are added, and then tipped out, one at a time.

4. The film is washed and hung to dry. The developed film is called a **negative**. This is because the dark and light tones are reversed.

5. Next, the printing process begins. The negative is put in an enlarger. This shines a larger, sharper version of each image on to a sheet of light-sensitive paper.

6. The paper (now called a **print**) is put in a chemical. Gradually, the image appears.

7. It is put in other chemicals, rinsed, and hung to dry.

Some darkrooms are lit with a safe light. A safelight is a red or orange light that does not ruin the paper used for printing black-and-white photographs.

Amazing black and whites

Black-and-white photographs are often more impressive than color photographs. The shapes and shadows stand out. The contrast between black shadows and white highlights is dramatic.

Tetons and Snake River was taken by American photographer Ansel Adams.

Ansel Adams

Photographer Ansel Adams (1902–1984) knew there was more to taking a photograph than pressing a button. He once said, "You don't take a photograph, you make it."

From Camera to Newsroom

A photograph can be taken, processed, and printed within minutes. But this is only possible with the help of a **digital camera** and computers. **Photojournalists** use these to get the latest news photographs to newspaper offices.

From camera to newspaper

If there is an earthquake somewhere in the world, photojournalists rush to get the latest photographs to newspaper editors. Here is a typical time line of what might happen:

1:00 p.m.—earthquake in Indonesia

2:00 p.m.—local photojournalist arrives in the damaged village and takes photographs

2:10 p.m.—uploads photographs to a laptop

2:11 p.m.—photographs sent by satellite to newspaper office in New York

2:13 p.m.—photographs are received and passed to picture department

2:30 p.m.—photograph is selected and edited on computer

2:35 p.m.—photograph is sent to printers for front page of newspaper

5:00 p.m.—evening edition of newspaper goes on sale.

A satellite dish transmits photographs from a laptop to the other side of the world in seconds.

Photographs may need to be cropped to fit a space on a newspaper page.

Photograph editing

You can change a photograph completely by using a computer and a photo editing program. Colors can be altered, people deleted, objects added, and so on. In photojournalism, the editing is usually minor. For example, sections of a photograph might be cropped, or cut off.

You decide

Should photographs for newspapers be edited or changed at all? Here are some different views.

Yes:
• Newspapers need good photographs so people will buy them.
• Photographs are like paintings, there is nothing wrong with improving them.

No:
• Photographs should tell the truth—they should be exactly what the photographer saw.
• If photographs are changed, how can we believe what we see?

Digital Camera Controls

Digital cameras are very popular. They are easy to use, but a lot of people never find out about everything they can do. The controls shown here are some of the most useful ones. The controls and symbols on other models may be different. To make the most of a digital camera, you should read the instruction manual.

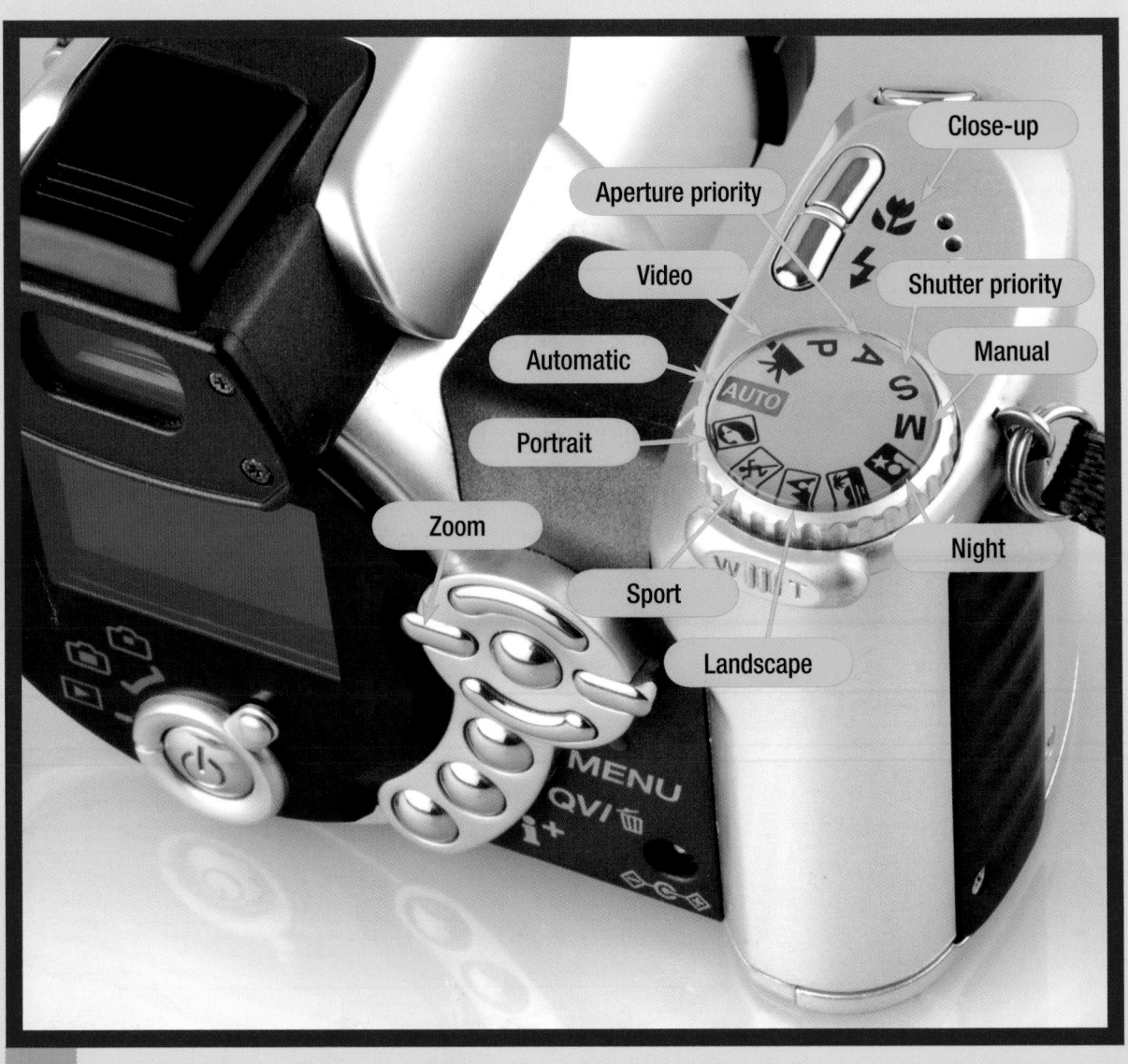

Aperture priority: Set the **aperture** you want (on a bright day, a smaller aperture will let in less light; on a darker day, a larger aperture will let in more light).

Picture with zoom

Automatic: The camera sorts out the **flash** and focus for you. All you do is point and click!

Close-up: Use this if the **subject** is closer than about 60 centimeters (24 inches).

Picture without zoom

Landscape: Use this for distant subjects, such as landscapes— just like the mountains in the symbol.

Manual: Use when you want to control the **exposure**.

Night: Use for nighttime photographs or when the subject is in dark shadows.

Overexposure

Portrait: Use for people and head-and-shoulder shots when the background is not important.

Shutter priority: Set the shutter speed you want (use a slower shutter speed for darker days and a faster shutter speed for moving objects, or they will look blurred).

Sport: This is not just for fast-moving sports—use it for any moving objects, such as birds or cars.

Portrait

Video: For taking a short video.

Zoom: This will operate the zoom **lens** (if you have one). Use it to get closer to your **subject**.

Shutter priority

The Perfect Photograph

How do you take a good photograph? First, it is important to learn to use a camera. Read the instructions and get to know how to use the controls. Then choose your **subject** carefully.

Composition

Photography is an art, and some photographs are put in **galleries**. Like paintings, they should show interesting colors, lines, and shapes.

To compose a photograph you must decide where to position different parts. Avoid putting your subject in the center. If it is a third of the way down from the top or a third of the way up, it will be much more interesting. This is known as the "rule of thirds."

This photograph of a zebra in Africa is by Frans Lanting.

Focal point

Every photograph must have a focal point—the part that catches the viewer's eye. Make sure it is clear and uncluttered.

Steady hands

Holding the camera steady while you take a photograph is essential. If you find this too difficult, use a **tripod**.

Ernst Haas

This Austrian photographer is well known for his use of color and experiments with light. He called himself "a painter in a hurry." This photograph shows the lights of Tokyo, Japan, reflected in a wet street.

Ernst Haas took this photograph during a trip to Japan in 1984.

Frans Lanting

This Dutch nature photographer tries to get close enough to wild animals to take amazing photographs. In the photograph on page 24, he has used the rule of thirds by placing his subject a third of the way down the photograph. There is also nothing to distract you from the focal point.

Light

Outdoors, if you want your subject fully lit, check that the sun is behind you. Taking a photograph while facing the sun can cause problems, unless you have a filter. Sunlight from the side can cast interesting shadows. Dramatic weather can cause light and shadows, too. Indoor photographs can use natural light from a large window. This gives a softer light than the harsh, direct light of a **flash**.

Choose your moment

Light and shadows change during the day. Try taking the same image, such as a tree, from the same place early in the morning, mid-morning, at noon, and at sunset. The varying light will affect the colors and shadows. You will end up with four very different photographs.

Annie Leibovitz finds a good spot to photograph Barack Obama at his inauguration in Washington, D.C.

Annie Leibovitz

A lot of photographers have become famous for portraits. American photographer Annie Leibovitz takes portraits of celebrities. She uses complex lighting, such as flash outdoors.

Gallery shot

Still-life paintings have been popular since the 1600s. They are paintings of carefully placed objects. Usually the objects are inanimate (not alive or moving). This activity challenges you to compose a still-life photograph using objects from the past.

Steps to follow:

1. Gather objects from a specific time in history, such as the 1800s, the 1960s, or perhaps the time when you were born. You could include clothes, jewelry, ornaments, toys, and even pictures.

2. Choose the most interesting objects from what you gathered, and try placing them next to one another. Look through your camera and keep moving the objects until you get the **composition** you want.

3. When you are happy, take several photographs from different angles and distances.

4. Make **prints** of your favorite shots.

5. Show your photographs to your friends. Can they guess how old the objects are?

Some tips

- Don't forget to choose the focal point. One or two items should stand out.
- Flash is not always necessary if you are working inside—light from a window can be very effective.
- If you have a computer and photo editing software available, try cropping your favorite photograph.

Far-Out Photography

Photographers work all around the world, taking photographs of people, places, animals, and events. Astronauts take photographs in space. Controllers on the ground use cameras on satellites (spaceships that orbit Earth) to take photographs of distant planets, stars, and galaxies.

Photographers often work in dangerous or difficult conditions. They have to take photographs in war zones, in the shadow of erupting volcanoes, or in areas where there are dangerous animals nearby.

Sports photographer Leo Mason captured this elegant jump by three gymnasts at the Beijing Olympics in 2008.

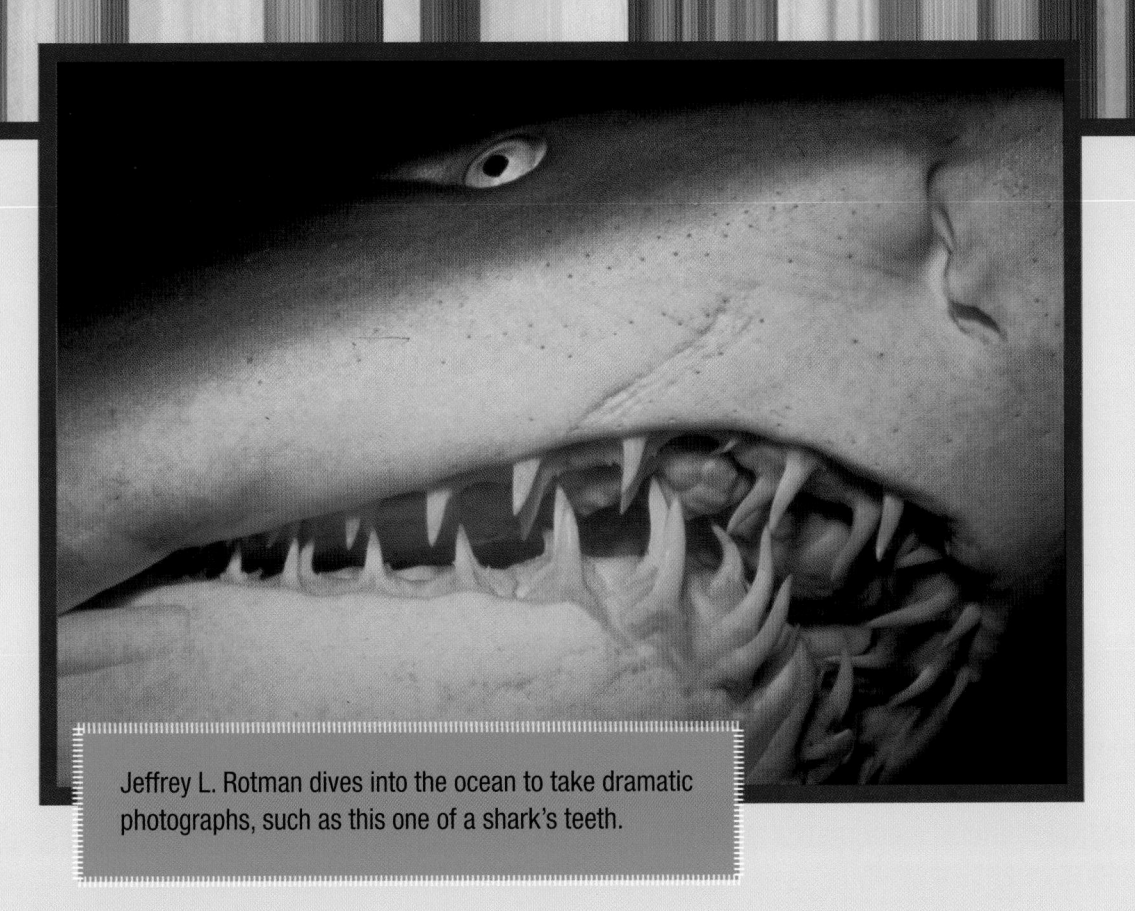

Jeffrey L. Rotman dives into the ocean to take dramatic photographs, such as this one of a shark's teeth.

Photographers often have a mission. It could be helping to sell a product or pointing out an injustice (unfairness) in the world. Wildlife photographers show us rare animals, and remind us to help protect the natural world.

Photography jobs

What kind of photographer would you choose to be, and why? Which photographers have the most important or interesting jobs? Discuss this question with your friends. Here are a few different types of photographer, and the things they try to do:

- Wildlife photographers—show animals that are in danger of extinction
- Fashion photographers—show new clothing that designers want to sell
- Art photographers—help people see beauty in the world, or to look at the world with a more critical eye
- **Photojournalists**—tell real-life stories and reveal problems in the world.

Glossary

amateur person who does something for fun or as a hobby

aperture hole in a camera the size of a pin, through which light enters

chemical substance made up of atoms and molecules

composition what you include and how you arrange things in a photograph

darkroom room where photographs are developed and printed

develop process film so that the images on it can be printed

digital camera camera that takes and stores images digitally

digital signal information in the form of numbers that computers understand

exposure amount of light that is allowed to enter a camera and be recorded on the film or light sensor

flash bright light that flashes on a camera, which lightens the photograph

gallery building where art, including photographs, is shown

LCD screen large screen on the back of a digital camera

lens glass that sharpens an image

light-sensitive picks up light. The film in a camera is light-sensitive.

light sensor part of a digital camera that detects light and makes it into an image

memory card card that goes in a digital camera on which photographs are saved

negative image in which the colors are reversed, so black areas look white

organ part of the body that has a particular function

photographic film paper that picks up light when a camera takes a photograph

photojournalist professional photographer who takes news images

pixel square of color, many of which make up a digital photograph

plate hard sheet on which photographic images can be recorded

portable something that can be carried around

positive image in which the colors are not reversed

print image that has been printed on paper

professional someone who makes money

snapshot photograph that has been taken quickly, without much planning

subject person or object in a photograph

tripod stand with three legs used to support a camera

viewfinder part of the camera you look through

Find Out More

Books

Buckingham, Alan. *Digital Photo Magic*. New York: Dorling Kindersley, 2005.

Gaines, Thom. *Digital Photo Madness!: 50 Weird and Wacky Things to Do with Your Digital Camera*. New York: Lark, 2006.

Hosack, Karen. *Photography*. Chicago: Raintree, 2009.

Websites

http://animals.nationalgeographic.com/animals
This site has some amazing wildlife photography.

www.photographymuseum.com/
This online museum showcases different exhibitions related to photography.

Famous photographer websites:

www.anseladams.com
Ansel Adams (black and white)

www.leomason.com
Leo Mason (sport)

www.muenchphotography.com
David Muench (nature)

Place to visit

George Eastman House
900 East Avenue
Rochester, NY 14607
Tel: (585) 271-3361
Eastman House has hundreds of thousands of photographs that document the history of photography.

Index